BOUNDARIES

BOUNDARIES

Protecting Yourself
from
Emotional Harm

RAYMOND LLOYD RICHMOND, PH.D.

First Edition September 2018
  Revised May 2019

Cover design by Raymond Lloyd Richmond, Ph.D.

ISBN-13: 978-1726375931

ISBN-10: 1726375935

CONTENTS

1   Boundaries 7

2   A False Belief 9

3   Boundaries Derive From Love 10

4   The Lack of Boundaries 12

5   Examples 14

6   Putting It Into Practice 17

7   Responsibility 20

8   Enemies of Love 32

9   Summary 35

10   Questions About Boundaries In Psychotherapy 38

    Index 61

    About the Author 67

1   BOUNDARIES

Always treat others with respect and dignity, even if you do not agree with them. But if they treat you with a lack of respect and dignity, then it's important for you to protect yourself with healthy boundaries.

By definition, a boundary is anything that marks a limit. A psychological boundary defines personal dignity. When we say to someone, "You just crossed a line," we are speaking about a psychological limit that marks the distinction between behavior that does not cause emotional harm and behavior that causes emotional harm.

We all need to protect ourselves from emotional harm. Psychological defenses are created in childhood to serve that purpose unconsciously, but they can also lead us into unhealthy and unproductive behavior. Boundaries, unlike psychological defense mechanisms, are conscious and healthy ways to protect ourselves from emotional harm.

The ideal of life is mutual cooperation, but if you must interact with others who are not cooperative and rather are hostile or manipulative then it is necessary to have strong boundaries to protect yourself.

Some persons, however, have great difficulty setting boundaries—they may even believe that setting boundaries is rude—and this difficulty usually derives from child abuse. But let's be clear that abuse can range from subtle emotional manipulation to severe sexual and physical abuse. To the unconscious, though, any abuse, no matter how mild or severe, is an insult to personal dignity.

It's precisely this insult to personal dignity that explains why adults who were abused as children lack the ability to set appropriate boundaries. As odd as it sounds, their *not having boundaries* served them as a defense mechanism in childhood. Most abused children know intuitively that if you try to do anything to resist the abuse, you just get hurt all the more. So setting aside any resistance means less hurt.

Sadly, defenses that served you very well as a child to ensure your survival can actually cripple you with fear, dishonesty, and self-sabotage when carried into adulthood. With persistence and courage, however, any psychological defense can be overcome. So if a lack of boundaries has gotten you into trouble in the past, take heart, for the problem can be remedied.

2   A FALSE BELIEF

First it will be important to overcome the pernicious belief that you are worthless. Like any frightened child you created this belief unconsciously to tolerate your lack of resistance to childhood mistreatment. The psychological logic is this: if you can convince yourself that you're worthless and therefore don't deserve any protection from degradation, then you can more easily justify not resisting anything that degrades your value.

Note carefully, though, that the belief that you are worthless is a negative belief that you created yourself; therefore you can just as well create another, positive belief to replace the negative belief. As a first step, you might begin this process by repeating to yourself, over and over, "I am not worthless." So let's continue from there.

3   BOUNDARIES DERIVE FROM LOVE

Healthy boundaries derive from love, not from fear. For example, you will often see so-called "nice" persons who always appear to sacrifice themselves for others. They give the impression that capitulating to others promotes peace and that boundaries are selfish—but many of these persons are motivated by an unconscious need to keep the "peace" because of their fear of conflict. Such persons usually come from dysfunctional families, where they may have played the unconscious family role of "peace keeper." They're angry at their parents, they feel guilty for being angry, and they fear any conflict that might reveal the truth about their anger. The real motive for their "nice" behavior, then, is fear, not love.

On the other hand, you can find persons who, knowing full well that they are being hurt, will sometimes set aside their boundaries as an act of charity for others. For example, if people push past you to get on a bus, you might decide to say nothing, knowing that people who would push past you to get on a bus will also react with hostility if you say anything to them about their rude behavior. In this case you can set aside your boundaries and tolerate their rude behavior with forbearance, praying that they might someday learn to act with charity to others. Yet the same persons who can willingly set aside their boundaries can just as well defend them. For example, if someone at work uses foul language, you can state that you do not like to hear such talk; if the talk persists, you can get up and walk away.

Thus there is a big difference between someone who has clear boundaries and is willing to protect them—and who can willingly set the boundaries aside for the good of others when necessary—and someone who, because of fear, tolerates anything. Therefore, acting out of fear only leads to a wasted life because it unconsciously supports rudeness and disorder. Acting from love, however, can bring genuine good into the world through your personal example. But only with healthy boundaries can you act from love. Let's see why this is so.

4   THE LACK OF BOUNDARIES

Consider that boundaries have a fundamental place in life itself. Look around you, and you will see that every living creature has its own territory which it defends against intrusion. Boundaries are so fundamental that even criminals who thrive on violating the integrity of others have their own internal code of ethics, their own "boundaries."

Considering, then, that boundaries have a core purpose in civilization, an individual's lack of personal, psychological boundaries isn't really a true lack—at least, it's not a lack in the philosophical sense of something "missing." Instead, this apparent lack is really a *refusal* to defend one's own dignity, and it's a refusal based on hatred. This hatred, though, is double-edged: it's a hatred for the self as well as a hatred for others.

It's a hatred for the self that results from living always in fear because of having been mistreated or abused as a child. Unable to make sense of senseless hurt, a child, using its best, but still imperfect, childhood logic, arrives at the only "logical" conclusion: "It's all my fault. I'm just a worthless person. I deserve condemnation for being worthless, and I deserve condemnation for always being so afraid." And there you have it: self-hatred caused by fear that is caused by abuse.

All of this self-hatred, however, derives from a hatred for others. For example, when a child is mistreated by a parent, the child will be angry with the parent, but, because it will feel dangerous to be angry with someone the child depends on for food and shelter, the child will hide the anger—and hate—by turning it against itself. Nevertheless, as hidden as it may be, the original focus of the anger is on the parent, not the on self.

That hidden hatred, therefore, hurts others as well as yourself. When others mistreat you now, as an adult, your dignity is insulted, yes, but by keeping quiet and allowing the mistreatment, you deprive them of what would essentially be a psychological warning about their social impropriety; that is, if you were to defend your boundaries and speak up about the mistreatment, you would at least give the offender the opportunity to recognize and repent the hurtful behavior.

To re-establish healthy boundaries, then, endeavor to stop *refusing* to defend boundaries. You can do this by starting to refuse to hate—and that includes refusing to hate or defile yourself.

5   EXAMPLES

To help you understand the range of reasons for having boundaries, here are some examples of healthy boundaries.

Refusing to break the law.

The law is absolute to a particular city, state, or country. Breaking the law is not just an act of hatred to authority, it is a criminal act with unpleasant penalties. If you break the law, even if others manipulate you into doing it, you are the one who has to pay the price. Getting yourself into trouble like this defiles everyone.

Refusing to bend the rules.

Unlike the law, which is absolute, rules of conduct are relative to a particular social context. Rules allow things to function smoothly because everyone within a particular context agrees to them. Rules can refer to a game, to office procedures, to family conduct, or even to the celebration of liturgy. But if you allow rules to be bent, then the whole social context becomes defiled.

Refusing to betray your moral values.

Your moral values provide your own internal guidance about something that is wrong to do, even if it might be legal or even if society encourages it. Moral values derive from an abstract sense of the "good," which has its origin in God. If you betray your moral values, such as by allowing yourself to be pressured into doing something immoral, you betray God and defile the good.

Refusing to allow someone to pressure you to get too close to you emotionally.

We do not live in a world of true love; we live in a world of selfishness, where others try to get their needs met even at the expense of your needs. People will try to get you to "open up" when you don't want to, they will try to get you to "spill your guts" when it can be used against you, they will try to get you to participate in activities that make you feel uncomfortable, and they will try to manipulate you to serve their needs.

Being pressured and manipulated like this defiles love, and allowing yourself to be pressured and manipulated like this defiles your love for yourself.

Refusing to subject your body to indignity.

We are physical creatures. Our bodies are made of bones and flesh. Each of us has a physical presence that makes us unique and contributes to our sense of individuality. Your body, therefore, needs to be protected with dignified behavior and clothing.

Therefore, dressing in a fashion that lacks dignity, allowing your body to be touched when you don't want to be touched, or allowing your health to be threatened (for example, smoking cigarettes or breathing second-hand cigarette smoke, eating junk foods, using drugs, or abusing alcohol) defiles your body and your dignity.

6   PUTTING IT INTO PRACTICE

The purpose of boundaries is not to tell others what to do or to control the behavior of others. Boundaries have the simple purpose of protecting yourself. There are two ways to use boundaries to protect yourself: one way is a matter of protecting yourself from what others *want from you*, and the other way is a matter of protecting yourself from what others *do to you*.

PROTECTING YOURSELF FROM WHAT OTHERS WANT FROM YOU: *SAYING "NO."*

It can be hard to say "No", but knowing that it is healthy to do so can make it easier. Here are some examples.

- I cannot do that right now; I will get to it in due time.

- I prefer not to discuss this right now.

- That's a private matter that I don't want to speak about.

- This isn't your responsibility; I'll take care of it myself.

- It's none of your business.

  (*This is a legitimate response if it is said gently and calmly and with a smile.*)

- I understand what you want, and yet it's against my values, and so I will not do it.

- I've already explained my opinion about the matter; I don't want to discuss it further.

- I have already said "No," and I'm not going to argue with you about it.

  (*If the other person keeps making objections, then just keep repeating, after every objection, "I said I'm not going to argue with you."*)

PROTECTING YOURSELF FROM WHAT OTHERS DO TO YOU: *STATING CONSEQUENCES.*

Note that if you tell others what to do, it will lead to opposition and conflicts. Therefore, the most effective strategy is to make statements in which you state what *you* will do if the other person does something contrary to your preferences. Here are some examples.

- I'm not going to listen to anything said with rudeness,

but if you speak to me kindly I will be glad to listen to you. So go ahead, try saying it again, but with gentleness.

- If you don't stop yelling at me, then I will hang up the phone.

- If you don't stop using foul language, then I will get up and leave.

- I've told you that I don't want you to keep sending me dozens of messages, so if you keep sending them I will delete them without reading them.

- If you send any more offensive text messages, then I will block your number.

- If you're going to complain about how I drive, then I will stop the car and won't drive any farther until you get out or be quiet.

- If you intend to dress like that, then I won't go with you.

- Listen, there's a complicating factor here that you're not aware of. [*Specify.*] I'm just trying to clarify things. If you're going to be sarcastic and call me stupid, then I'm not going to help you with this task.

7 RESPONSIBILITY

In the process of developing boundaries, it is necessary to consider the related matter of *responsibility*. Many persons grow up without learning to assume proper responsibility for their own lives, and so they can have an attitude of entitlement and rudeness to others, even to the point of bullying and terrorism. Thus we all need strong, healthy boundaries to protect ourselves from those persons who can be dangerous to us.

On the other hand, many persons grow up believing that they are responsible for the feelings of others, and so they will resist even the desire to have boundaries because they believe that someone who asserts boundaries is being mean and rude to others.

Consequently, to have healthy boundaries we need a clear understanding of the meaning of *responsibility*.

Responsibility For Your Own Life

To take responsibility for your own life means two things. First, taking responsibility for your own life means to endeavor to stop blaming others for anything that befalls you. It means that no matter what pain or suffering is inflicted on you, you have an obligation to pay the price yourself for its remedy. No matter what your parents—or anyone—ever did to you, still you have an obligation to work in the present to achieve your healing.

> Even self-loathing and self-punishment—even to the point of suicide—are all veiled forms of blaming others as a way to avoid facing up to the truth of your emotional pain, and, therefore, they are all veiled forms of avoiding your own healing.

Second, taking responsibility for your own life means to endeavor to assume personal liability for the injurious consequences of your actions. The true acceptance of this responsibility will lead to feelings of sorrow, and this sorrow, if accepted without falling into the trap of self-punishment, will lead to the desire to do anything it takes to alter your behavior. To shirk this responsibility, however, will lead you into the dead-end trap of victimization.

Victimization

In the ancient sense of the word, *victim* means an animal

offered in sacrifice. These sacrificial animals, however, did not offer themselves—they were taken from the flocks—and so, through the ages, the term victim became associated with the idea of someone who (a) loses something against his will or (b) is cheated or duped by another. Consequently, in modern society, the ancient meaning of a victim has been lost to us, and our use of the term carries with it all the unconscious resentment we feel for being cheated, duped, or unfairly treated. In essence, according to today's language, a victim is someone who has been victimized.

So, when we call someone a victim today we imply that the person suffered unwillingly and unfairly; moreover, according to modern sensibilities, we assume that this injustice deserves some social compensation. If the compensation does not come freely, we demand it. We sue. We protest. We kill. We fall into victim anger.

This very attitude—this bitterness and resentment for having been treated unfairly—is a poison that prevents emotional wounds from healing. It stunts the psychological and spiritual qualities of patience, understanding, compassion, forbearance, mercy, and forgiveness that are necessary for emotional healing.

> Some individuals, however, will avoid the work of their psychological healing because they incorrectly believe that admitting the truth about others' lack of caring amounts to blaming those persons. But

healing depends on admitting the truth, whatever it may be. To deny the truth only drives resentments out of sight into the unconscious. Hence it can be that those who hide the truth to protect others from blame lock themselves into an unconscious blame which prevents them from taking responsibility for their own lives. Thus, even as they tell themselves that their lives are failures, they really have succeeded at something : they have become successful at blaming others while hiding that fact from themselves.

A Question

I am puzzled by something you wrote. You claim that in order to change, a person must feel sorrow for the pain he or she has inflicted on others—and to no longer blame others. That makes sense regarding instances where we injure others; but I am reading from the perspective of someone whose parents were verbally abusive and emotionally negligent, who is now trying to recognize the feelings and beliefs buried in childhood. While adults should consider whether their abusive parent(s) might have suffered child abuse (leading to their own feelings of unworthiness), do you expect a victim of child abuse to feel responsible for sorrow felt by the parents/perpetrators and to not blame the abusive parents/perpetrators for the pain they inflicted ?

When I speak about psychological change, I'm addressing the person who wants to change. In your case, that's you.

If you were abused as a child, then you probably responded to the emotional pain of the abuse in various ways, including blame, resentment, and anger. Now, as an adult, the sorrow you may feel for all the mistakes you made in the past can motivate you to change your behavior.

In regard to the abuse that was inflicted on you as a child, your healing depends on your understanding that the abuse was not your fault and that you were not responsible for the behavior of those who abused you. Your abusers had their own reasons for acting as they did, but that's their responsibility. Someday they might feel sorrow for what they did, and, even though it may seem unlikely, they might even apologize to you some day. But you are neither responsible for making them feel sorrow nor for mitigating the pain of any sorrow they might feel. Their sorrow, if they have any at all, is their own responsibility. The only thing you can do to help them is refuse to hate them, because your hatred will drive them deeper into their own denial.

Eventually, as your healing progresses, and you understand yourself better than you do now, you may be able to understand your abusers better; this is called *empathy*. Empathy is a good thing, but it can't be rushed. If you try to force yourself into feeling empathy before you're ready for it, then it won't have any meaning other than that of a distraction from real healing.

Finally, it's important to understand something about

blame. Being open to acknowledge the facts of what afflicted you as a child is necessary for your healing. For the sake of psychological honesty, it's important to be able to state the facts of your childhood objectively and without prejudice, such as, "They did this or that," or "They failed me." It's also important to be honest about how those parental failures hurt you and inhibited your psychological growth. But stating facts like this is not a matter of blaming your parents.

In *blame* you don't just state the facts, you gloat over them, clinging to your resentment of others in the unconscious hope that, in your making a big enough stink about it, maybe your abusers will suffer for what they did. Blame is a mistake, though, because when you cling to resentment you keep your focus on what "they did," rather than putting your focus on what you can do to reclaim your life *despite* what "they did."

When you let go of blame you let go of the belief that it's your responsibility to bring justice upon others by your making them suffer. Your responsibility is only to recover your dignity despite what others did to you, regardless of why they did it.

Practical Examples

To learn how to take responsibility for your own life, it can be helpful to distinguish several different aspects to

the concept of *responsibility*: recognizing your own imprudence, respecting the time of others, respecting a promise
you make, and not trying to protect others from their own
feelings.

Imprudence

There can be times when it is necessary to take responsibility for any loss or injury you cause because of your
imprudence.

- Let's say you make a reservation for an event that has a
  24 hour cancellation policy; that is, if you don't give at
  least 24 hours advance notice to cancel, you must still
  pay the fee. On the day of the event, you decide that you
  could do some errands before the event and still be able
  to arrive just at the start of the event. While doing the
  errands, you lose your wallet and your mobile phone.
  You fall into a panic as you try to deal with the loss,
  and you miss the event entirely. The next day you try
  to explain what happened and that your missing the
  event was not your fault. But you are still charged for
  the event. So, are you responsible for paying the charge
  even if you believe it's unfair?

  Yes, you are responsible. It was imprudence on your
  part to have expected that everything would go as you
  planned. You did not consider that anything could
  have gone wrong, and that your plans could have been
  thwarted. Had you been prudent, you would have con-

sidered the loss you might have incurred if you did not arrive on time for the event, and so you might have left more time between the errands and the event, or you might have scheduled the errands for some other time, such as after the event.

Respecting the Time of Others

There can be times when it is necessary to take responsibility for causing the loss of someone's time—and, by extension, for causing someone's financial loss as well—even if you were not imprudent.

- Let's say you make an appointment with someone who charges an hourly rate. He blocks out that time for you on his schedule and promises to wait for you. On the day of the appointment, you have a family emergency, and you forget about the appointment entirely. Several days later you try to explain to the man what happened and that your missing the appointment was not your fault. But he explains that he waited for you for the entire hour you had scheduled and that he is charging you for his time. So, are you responsible for paying?

  Yes, you are responsible. Certainly you suffered distress because of the family emergency, but this person suffered the loss of his time as well as a financial loss because you did not notify him that you would not keep the appointment.

Respecting a Promise You Have Made

There can be times when it is necessary to take responsibility for causing inconvenience to someone because you fail to keep a promise.

- Let's say you have promised to drive someone to the airport, but on the day of the flight some unforeseen obligation occurs and you have to change your plans. What do you do?

  You can take responsibility for your promise. You can tell the person what has occurred, and then you can offer to pay for—or, if necessary, even arrange for—any alternate form of transportation.

Despite what some persons might want to believe, the matter of keeping a promise is not an insignificant thing. In dysfunctional families, though, children will often say anything to appease their parents, and so the act of abusing the truth becomes commonplace for the children. Nevertheless, a broken promise is actually a betrayal of the truth.

Therefore, someone endeavoring to live a responsible life will maintain a constant scrutiny of anything he or she says and will resist any temptation to automatically say anything just to appease another person. In fact, this temptation to appease another person leads us to a point about false responsibility.

Not Taking Responsibility for the Thoughts and Behaviors of Others

There can be times when you cause distress and anxiety to yourself because you are always "walking on eggshells" in fear of how other persons will react to something you do or say.

- Let's say you are at work and someone brings in a plate of homemade baked goods. She holds out the plate proudly and asks you to have some. But you are careful about your health, and so you limit sweets and don't eat between meals—yet you are afraid of hurting her feelings. So what do you do?

  You can thank her for her efforts and say politely that you limit sweets and do not eat between meals. You are not wrong or cruel or insensitive for having boundaries and declining to eat anything you do not want. Your co-worker's feelings are her responsibility, not yours, and it's her responsibility to learn to cope with them in a psychologically healthy manner and to not get entangled in negative thoughts and behaviors related to you or to herself. If she tries to blame you because she feels rejected, then she is wrong, and you need the strength to resist her attempts to shirk responsibility for her life by pushing blame onto others or onto external circumstances.

Therefore, if you want to be healthy and take responsibility for your own life, then keep the focus on *your* life, not on the lives of others. Learn to recognize the many ways in which you can be tempted to shirk responsibility for your life by falling into the false belief that you must forsake your boundaries and take responsibility for the thoughts and behaviors of others out of an irrational fear of hurting their feelings.

In families where there is physical abuse, irrational outbursts of anger, or "discipline" that uses shaming to control children with fear, a child will be unconsciously trained to be wary of doing anything that might "cause" an unpleasant reaction in a parent. When these children become adults it can be difficult to overcome the fear of "hurting the feelings" of someone. *Ironically, these persons are really more afraid of getting hurt themselves than of hurting someone else.* That is, they are afraid that if they speak honestly then they will be shamed for being selfish or stupid, or that the other person will get angry.

To overcome such a childhood fear, the psychological task is to learn how to use healthy boundaries to cope with the dysfunctional behaviors of others rather than wrongly take blame for their behaviors.

Therefore, you don't have to fear speaking the truth even if someone might go into a silent sulk for several days or fly into a rage. You can let the other person sulk or fly into a rage, and you can stay calm about it, if only you remember one thing: the inappropriate behaviors of another are not caused by you, they are acts of free will on the part of the other; that is, they may be unconsciously motivated, but, if they become outward acts, a conscious choice has been made by the other to not restrain them. This lack of restraint is the fault of the other, not your fault. So have the courage to remain firm in protecting your boundaries and firm in not being manipulated with fear, guilt, and shame.

8   ENEMIES OF LOVE

What occurs when parents don't really want the good of their children? What occurs when parents constantly criticize their children, abuse them, and essentially stifle any good that the children could achieve? In short, what occurs in dysfunctional families when parents don't really love their children but manipulate and control them?

Well, parents such as this don't love their children and, to their children, that makes them enemies, not parents worthy of being honored. Trying to honor parents such as this amounts to trying to carry out a fraud. After all, how can you honor your enemies?

Consequently, the only relationship you can have with such persons—whether they be parents, siblings, or friends—is a relationship of truth. See the truth, then: understand that such persons do not love you. See it clearly.

If you don't see it, you will be endlessly trying to appease them, to do something to make them love you. You will be dependent on your hope for their love. You will be like a dog begging for scraps and dying of hunger because the scraps are not real food.

If you do see the truth, you will realize that making other persons love you is impossible. They will never love you unless they change psychologically; they will never love you unless they see the truth of their own brokenness and want to be healed.

You can't make them change, and you can't heal them yourself, but you can stop encouraging them to remain the same. So how do you stop encouraging them? Stop being nice.

The deep unconscious motive for being nice is fear, the fear that if you speak the truth you will offend someone who will then reject you and abandon you. To love is to speak the truth and, with non-judgmental bluntness, to call lies and errors, well, lies and errors.

> Imagine someone talking to a friend, complaining about how difficult it is to have problem children. If the friend were merely nice, the friend would say, "There, there, you're doing your best to be a good mother." But if the friend were to speak the truth, the friend would say, "Well, no wonder your children have so many problems! Look at how miserably cruel you are to them!"
>
> So there's the difference between being nice and speaking the truth from a heart filled with love.

So stop being nice and start being genuine.

To be genuine with others, though, you have to do your own psychological work first, so that you can be genuine with yourself. Once you can see how you deceive yourself, then you can help others see how they deceive themselves.

Mind you, being around anyone who is an enemy of love while you are still in the process of your own healing can be psychologically precarious and dangerous. Your best protection, at least temporarily, may be to distance yourself emotionally—and even physically if necessary—from any emotionally caustic person who is an enemy of love.

9   SUMMARY

Life often involves counter-intuitive principles. For example, to drive from one place to another you may have to drive for a while in a direction away from your destination.

Psychology, too, is like this. Boundaries can have a counter-intuitive element to them. When others make demands of you, you demonstrate that you care about others by resisting the temptation to cross certain boundaries in an attempt to fulfill the others' demands. To the other, your protection of your boundaries can feel restrictive—even confusing or rude—but to you it's a job well done.

The explanation for this can be found in the psychology of infant development.

The time of infancy brings with it the expectation that the child's expression of his or her needs will lead to the fulfillment of those needs. A child cries, and a mother—a good mother—will hasten to feed the child, change the diaper, relieve pain, or do whatever else must be done to attend to the child. After all, a good mother can interpret the meaning of any cry.

As infancy progresses into childhood, a new task begins. Rather than be dependent on having their needs fulfilled in all things, children learn how to fulfill their own needs. They want to hold their own cup and tie their own shoes. This prepares children to grow into mature and responsible adults.

In a dysfunctional family, however, little of this healthy learning takes place. If infants are denied the comfort of feeling understood, they will not be able to take up the task of wanting to fulfill their own needs. Never having felt understood, they will feel burdened by always having to take care of themselves. The mature obligation of fulfilling their own needs as adults will seem like a curse.

Consequently, if you acquiesce to the temptation to give to others everything they want, you will infantilize them. Instead of being an example of mature confidence and independence, you will psychologically cripple others. If you make this mistake, you show that you do not really care about others.

> In a similar way, psychotherapy offers the opportunity
> to learn as an adult what was not learned naturally in
> childhood. In psychotherapy, clients can experience
> the comfort of being understood. Clients can speak
> about the needs they have, they can feel the yearning

to have those needs fulfilled, and they can verbalize the pain of not having someone else fulfill those needs. Being honest about this pain, and feeling understood in expressing it, clients can then learn confidently to take up tasks that previously felt oppressive.

If, however, the psychotherapist acquiesces to the demand to fulfill the client's needs, the attempt will infantilize the client, will overwhelm the psychotherapist, and will lead to a failure of the psychotherapy. Instead of teaching the client mature independence, the psychotherapist will cripple the client. A psychotherapist who makes this mistake shows that he or she does not really care about the client.

Thus the full irony becomes revealed: only by maintaining your boundaries can you give real love to others.

10 QUESTIONS ABOUT BOUNDARIES IN PSYCHOTHERAPY

My concern is that my new psychotherapist of about 5 months has told me she suffers from depression and an anxiety disorder, takes antidepressant medication, and has told me about her emotionally distant mother. Is this OK for me? My previous psychotherapist of many years died unexpectedly and was reluctant to say much about herself unless it was more in context of helping me. I like this new psychotherapist a lot. She has helped me through the grieving process, and obviously cares about my mental health. I have clinical depression and anxiety. She knows what I am feeling; it's obvious she knows not just because of book learning but because she has had similar feelings. Do I need to be concerned about her boundaries?

Using good clinical judgment, a psychotherapist can at times set aside therapeutic neutrality and use self-disclosure as a clinical tool to inspire and encourage a client. For example, imagine if a psychotherapist were to say something like this: "I came from a dysfunctional family and suffered emotionally as a child with self-doubt and uncertainty and had periods of depression. Through my studies and through my own psychotherapy I learned to overcome my resentments at my parents, my unconscious anger, my victim mentality, and my experiences of depression—and I did it all without any psychiatric medication. So I'm fully prepared to help you do the same."

That would be inspiring, wouldn't it? But your psychotherapist didn't do that. Instead, she self-disclosed her failure.

Your psychotherapist essentially told you that she was unable to get to the unconscious core of her problems and has resigned herself to suppressing her symptoms with medication. There's no encouragement in that outlook on life. Her "boundaries"—that is, her lack of boundaries—will fence you in rather than protect you from the dangers of the world.

So, will this so-called "psychotherapist" be of any therapeutic help for you? Well, it depends on what you want your life to become. If you want to get to the unconscious core of your symptoms and heal them, then you would be better served by someone who can offer you more hope than you have been offered in the last five months. But if you are content with merely suppressing symptoms and surviving—rather than living—then stay with what you have.

I have been seeing my psychotherapist for nearly eight years. We have had a very profound, intense relationship with varying degrees of transference and countertransference. At one point in treatment we had to stop so that he could deal with his own issues and countertransference.

During treatment in order to help me with my eating disorder we began to have dinners together and talking outside of the office led to his sharing information with me about himself and another client with whom he was having difficulty. He has been a very important part of my life, and we have discussed friendship after therapy. I have seen him outside of the office for other occasions, always respecting the boundaries of therapy and for therapeutic reasons. Our conversations began to feel as if we were friends, and we would process this in therapy. He has always said that I did not come for friendship and I agreed. I have become very attached to him.

Recently this other client attempted suicide and on that particular day I was his first patient. I saw that he was a mess, and we talked about the situation instead of my having my session. So he revealed to me his turmoil and personal feelings.

A few weeks later he abruptly told me that he could not see me outside of the office and that our relationship would change. He could only see me for sessions and I could not leave him phone messages any longer as I had in the past.

At any rate, I have had an enormously emotional re-action to all this. We had some very hostile sessions and volatile exchange of words, raised voices, and nastiness. He is in supervision and I have felt betrayed, abandoned, angry, outraged, sad, depressed, and in total despair. I have continued my sessions with him with a two week break and he seems still torn apart my his inability to deal with this other client and to keep his boundaries clean.

I feel ripped off and still at odds with myself and him. When I see him this is all that we have talked about for the past month. I am starting to resent paying him and scared to stop treatment. I need some guidance here.

As sad as it is, your experience illustrates several points about psychotherapy and the psychology of the unconscious.

First, it makes clear the fact that psychotherapy with a student under supervision may be less expensive than treatment with an experienced professional, but it is not always competent psychotherapy. Now, I understand that students can learn only from direct experience—in fact, I had to learn this way myself—and so supervised training is an important part of a student's training; still, the consumer should be aware of the risks involved. Many students not only are caught up in their own personal issues but also they lack the sophisticated experience and boundaries necessary to avoid the unconscious traps into which clients can draw them. This points to the fact that only with precise boundaries can a professional perform a job well done.

This leads to the second point: your unconscious desire was to seduce—that is, to control—your psychotherapist. Let me explain. An eating disorder has its roots in the desire to "be in control." By controlling your own body both through food intake and through food expulsion (vomiting, laxatives, or exercise) you symbolically control your feelings of vulnerability and helplessness in not being able to control a parent who emotionally manipulated you. Thus, when you are motivated by the unconscious desire to be in control, all your relationships become stained with your need to control them—and it's no different with your psychotherapeutic relationship.

This leads to the third point: you can get drawn into a dysfunctional relationship because of an unconscious desire not just to control the other person but also to rescue the other person through "love". This love, though, is not true love—that is, the selfless giving of kindness, compassion, forbearance, and patience without asking for or expecting anything in return. No. This love that snared you is the common love of romantic fantasy, and it has at its core the desire to manipulate another person to get whatever you want—whether it be bodily pleasure, emotional security, financial security, social status, or any other personal satisfaction. In your case, your attachment to your psychotherapist derived from your unconscious desire to rescue him from his "mess." And what would you get from this desire? Well, you would get the symbolic satisfaction of reversing your father's inattention to you and of drawing him back to you emotionally through the person of your psychotherapist.

This leads to the fourth point: anger. Because it's unconsciously based in a desperation to feel accepted, and so is focused on the self, not on the other person, romantic love cannot cure childhood emotional wounds, and so it eventually must confront the frustration of its own failure. When that happens, common love flip-flops right into rage. You forget all about wanting to rescue the other, and you fall into the fury of wanting to "kill" him—that is, to get rid of him.

And this leads to the fifth point: guilt. Feeling so guilty about the effects of your anger, you remain tangled in a dysfunctional relationship; that is, because you believe that the other person needs you, and that protecting your dignity with healthy boundaries would be cruel, you stifle your hurt and continue to put up with abuse.

So what can you do?

Well, you can realize that now you know what psychotherapy isn't. It isn't the process of acting out any of the above points. Once you know what it isn't, then you can seek out real psychotherapy with someone who won't let you seduce him. A competent psychotherapist has good boundaries and won't let you get entangled with him like any other person. He won't create the illusion that he is your friend and confidant. Instead, he will reveal to you your unconscious. He will help you feel the pain of having been manipulated like an object when you were a child, and he will help you learn how to let go of your unconscious need to control the world. In all of this, you will learn real love and forgiveness—and then you will be "fixed." You will be freed of the illusion that the other person needs you to rescue him. You will be freed of the allure of dysfunctional relationships. You will be freed of your rage at your father.

Go back, therefore, to the first point and find a competent psychotherapist. Then work through the other points properly: instead of acting them out, speak them within the process of real psychotherapy.

Finally, there is one irony to be pointed out here. Whatever you need to in your psychotherapy now is what your so-called psychotherapist failed to do in his own psychotherapy (that is, if he ever had any). After all, this whole mess started because he lacked boundaries and was entangled in the illusion that he needed to rescue you.

Yes, I am in love with my psychotherapist, so maybe my perceptions are biased or delusional, but at the same time I feel violated and disrespected and that I am being driven to secondary insanity.

A few months ago, when he told me that he was leaving on vacation, I mentioned how difficult it is when he is gone. He replied, "You should just come to [...]. It's not a bad idea." The following week during the same scenario he replied, "You should just come with me. We could spend some time, you know, talking about [expletive deleted]" No, he didn't mean what he was saying, but the lightness of these comments felt demeaning.

We spend large portions of our sessions in casual conversation, sometimes up to half. Once, when I stated we had wasted to much of our session he replied, "That's what happens when you have relationships that only lasts one hour a week." A few weeks ago after we had spent fifty minutes visiting I asked how much time we had left and he answered, "Ten minutes. Why? Did you want to talk about things?" He says that he thinks psychotherapy should be personal, and that feelings of closeness and caring are to be expected. After working as a nurse aid for the past ten years, I understand the importance of respecting feelings that my patients have for me, and the importance of preventing confusion around those feelings—and I'm just a dumb bed-maker. As I stated at the beginning, maybe my infatuation is clouding my vision, but this behavior seems to resemble that of the annoying guys who follow me around the grocery store asking me if I have a boyfriend and what my phone number is. I understand that rules regarding boundaries in psychotherapy are open to a wide range of interpretations, but are there any circumstances under which this behaviour would be considered normal?

Are there any circumstances under which this behavior would be considered normal? Yes. In a grocery store.

Psychotherapy, however, is different from shopping for groceries—or seduction.

One basic tenet of psychoanalysis and psychodynamic psychotherapy asserts that, until we have reached a relatively deep state of psychological awareness, unresolved emotional conflicts from childhood will unconsciously motivate all the interpersonal interactions we have in the present. So, yes, even though your feelings for your psychotherapist are genuine, they still derive from unresolved feelings from your past, most likely about your father. Your psychotherapist could give you all the comfort of casual conversation and light comments in the world, but it would never be enough, and it would never heal your inner pain. Why? Because you really yearn for your father's comfort which, as a result of all his emotional failures, you never received. And in that frustrated yearning you feel tremendous hurt and become angry.

Your task, then, is to keep looking at the present with an eye to the past. You have to come to terms with your father's failures. You need to look at them honestly—without shame or malice—and see clearly how much you were hurt and how much those emotional wounds still live within you, in all things, to this day.

Once you start this task, honestly, in small bits here and there, you can begin the broader effects of healing: to give to others the comfort that you never received as a child.

But you need a psychotherapist who can guide you competently into this process. Now, if your psychotherapist said the things you say he said, in exactly the way you say he said them, then his casualness misses the point about true psychotherapy. In his lack of boundaries, he could be taking his own unconscious frustrations and cynicism out on you.

It often happens, however, that a psychotherapist might seem to be making idle conversation when really he is "poking around" looking for unconscious clues to the client's experiences. In medicine, when a physician examines your body with a stethoscope, this is called auscultation (from the Latin *auscultare*, to listen), and in a similar way a psychotherapist will be listening for significant hints of the unconscious in the casual things you say.

Also, when a psychotherapist points out an unpleasant aspect of a client's behavior, the client can become confused and upset and can even project his or her own feelings of anger onto the psychotherapist; thus the client will end up believing that the psychotherapist is angry and purposely saying hurtful things. This is transference in its most destructive aspects.

For the client, though, it can be almost impossible to tell whether feelings about the psychotherapy are based in transference or whether they are based in genuinely inappropriate behavior of the psychotherapist. Thus the psychotherapist's entire demeanor must be considered. If the psychotherapist is always professional and considerate, and has good boundaries, then a client's feelings of being dismissed are likely transference reactions. But if, even in a joking way, the psychotherapist ever suggests something unethical—such as going on vacation with him—or if he never links seemingly idle chit-chat in one part of a session to a later psychodynamic interpretation, then it's time for the client to beware.

I have been in psychotherapy for eight years. I saw my first psychotherapist for four years until she left the practice; we worked towards an ending over a period of months, and I started to see a psychotherapist from the same practice shortly afterwards.

I have been seeing my current psychotherapist for four years. Two weeks ago I had difficulty talking to my psychotherapist as we had been talking about some sexual abuse I suffered as a child, and I found it difficult to talk about it. I said, "This can't go on for ever can it?" And my psychotherapist said, "No it can't."

From there my psychotherapist started talking about endings and said maybe I needed to set an ending to the psychotherapy.

I said I did not want to do this and she persisted and suggested a time frame of six months. I have talked to her about it and said whilst I realise that the psychotherapy cannot continue inevitably I do not feel ready to set a date.

She said that as we have started the process of ending the psychotherapy I have to set a date for ending or she will do it. When I asked why, she said that it is an issue of boundaries and that we have started the ending process and there is no going back.

My questions is why is this an issue of boundaries, and my psychotherapist cannot explain this to me. I feel that the psychotherapist wants to leave and that she is forcing me to end the psychotherapy so that the same thing doesn't happen as with the first psychotherapist.

I believe I can not untangle what is coming from me

and what is coming from my psychotherapist. She also implied that setting an end date was in my best interests and I don't agree. I don't know the best way to deal with this.

The key issue here can be found in your statement that "I feel that the psychotherapist wants to leave and that she is forcing me to end the psychotherapy so that the same thing doesn't happen as with the first psychotherapist."

The truth is, your treatment with your first psychotherapist ended when she left the practice. So does your current psychotherapist now have plans to leave the practice herself? Well, we don't know.

But we do know how you feel. Look to the emotional content of your statement. You feel that "she is forcing me to end the psychotherapy." Actually, this is a statement of belief, not feeling. To get to the feelings associated with this belief, we can say that you must feel pressured, confused, hurt, and abandoned. Furthermore, if you think about this a bit, that's exactly how a child feels when she is sexually abused.

So, given these feelings, are they coming from your unconscious past, or from your psychotherapist's veiled motives for ending your treatment? Well, the only way to untangle this mess is to ask her directly if she has plans to leave her practice. If she says that she is, in fact, planning to leave, then you know that your feelings are coming from her—that is, that you have intuitively perceived what she has failed to say openly.

If she denies that she has plans to leave, then that leaves you with a mess of its own. You then have to wonder why she is forcing an end to the treatment. Is it a matter of your insurance running out? Is she afraid to deal with sexual abuse issues? Is she frustrated that after spending eight years in treatment you still find it difficult to speak openly about the abuse?

Whatever her motive, she owes you an honest explanation. If she fails to give that explanation, then she is re-creating within the treatment the same sort of abuse that afflicted you as a child, leaving you with the same feelings now— and the same lack of boundaries and the same lack of respect for your needs—that you experienced as an abused child. In that case, it would be best for you to get away now, while you have the chance, and to find someone who can treat you according to your best interests.

I have been receiving help within the mental health system for much of my life. I have been diagnosed as having Borderline Personality Disorder. I have anxiety that grips me despite a lifetime of looking for spiritual or other answers to my mental an emotional suffering. I had a psychotherapist for 15 years; he recently retired.

He was very cruel in the last year, I don't understand why; he said things such as "You will probably take your serious condition to the grave," "You should have made more progress in 15 years," "There are patients worse than you." Why he said these things I am not clear even now. All this has left me unable to integrate or move on. Feel very hurt, angry, stuck. And my pain from the relationship ending (though I may have contact in the future after a 6 month+ break, he has said—though I have to admit I did badger him about contact) and being so hurtful/cruel leaves me feeling I need closure, a talk with him NOW, but I have to wait, he says.

I didn't realise how much I was actually "in love" with him until most recently, and it seems he flirted with me for most of 15 years with a cup of tea ready at the outset of each session—no other patient had that. He said I was "special" yet it seems like he never really cared about me and it seems I have fallen in love with him. Yet he seems to have just dumped me at the end of the therapy. At least he ignored in the last year all the e-mails I sent (we had e-mail contact between sessions) all the excruciating pain of in the erotic transference. I could not, when I was in the therapy room with him, express anger at him or get him to help me deal with all the feelings, and suffered mostly the anger and pain between sessions in the last year, and cannot now work it through because he no longer does psychotherapy.

I feel so let down by the mental health system. It feels it was sado-masochistic, and he often said he felt that sado-masochism would be an approach I should look towards. I wonder now about his own intentions towards me, and I have not enjoyed it at all, and I feel so damaged by him.

How can this be? I paid so much money, and I can barely survive on my benefits? And even struggle to survive? He kept talking about Nietzsche and how everything moves towards disintegration and therefore self-destruction is not a bad thing, but when I said I felt suicidal because of the way he was speaking to me he said that would make him angry. He talked a fair bit about his atheism, and this itself has disturbed me, and been unhelpful. He has criticised my spiritual inclinations, but more to the point, any spiritual understanding of life—which has always been very important to me.

He said lots of hurtful things to me like "You would have been better dealt with by the criminal justice system." When I said how hurt this phrase (and others I mentioned earlier) made me feel and how destructive his approach was being (in the last year), he just didn't deal with it, or help me deal with my feelings; my emails expressing hurt and pain and anger about his attitude, he just ignored 90% of the time. And in sessions I was so besotted with him and felt so happy to be there in his room, I found it hard to challenge him or express anger.

When I did on the phone for example, he was just angry and nasty back.

Yet I was clearly suffering so much and so distressed. I think, now, we had "just a cup of a tea and a chat" and no "real therapy" for 15 years—it seemed like more of a "real" relationship, and yet when I asked for contact after termination he said it has all been "just illusion." I trusted he knew what he was doing. I believe now he realised I was actually in love with him, but he seems clueless about the impact he has had on me. I really don't know what to do—I have had suicidal thoughts for some time about this matter regarding my psychotherapist and trying to find a way out of this mess. I don't believe people in the mental health system here have much insight or care for those they are paid to help. I cannot decide what to do, just know I am not coping well, and have been ill, mentally, emotionally and physically because of this situation. He would blame me, angrily, and say I am doing it to myself. (I see the point of this judgment to some extent, but still, surely I have been in psychotherapy to deal with this problem?) 15 years is a long time to have wasted and that is how it feels. I don't believe he has helped me, and I am so angry, and often feel like I cannot go on. Can you suggest how I might get help with this and go forward in a life that was already very, very difficult before I started seeing him 15 years ago, and now feels intolerable?

The core of the BPD dynamic is unresolved rage from

the emotional wounds of childhood. Accordingly, the psychotherapeutic treatment for BPD involves a psychological resolution of rage. This resolution is accomplished by bringing to conscious expression the emotions underlying the rage; in essence, this process discovers the unconscious meaning of the rage itself and thereby contains the raw experiences. It's a bit like taming a wild animal.

Now, in the psychotherapeutic process, it is inevitable that the client's anger will be brought out into the open from time to time. The psychologist, therefore, has the task of tolerating the client's anger without reacting to it with the natural response of revenge. The psychologist must always seek the meaning of the client's behavior—and bring that meaning out into the open so that the client can recognize it and learn from it. There is no room in this for retaliation.

In this regard, the psychotherapeutic process can be obstructed by two things.

1. The psychologist could attempt to appease the client. This usually occurs because the psychologist has an unconscious fear of the client and wants to escape an emotionally difficult experience. In clinical practice this appeasement manifests in the psychologist violating professional boundaries so as to make the client feel special.

2. The psychologist could react to the client's anger with

his or her own anger. This reaction contains an unconscious—or, sadly, even a conscious—desire to harm
the client. Quite often this reaction takes the form of
saying something that demeans or belittles the client,
and it's all based in an abuse of power that allows the
psychologist to recover from a feeling of helplessness
when confronted with an angry client.

With this introduction, we can understand how your experience with your psychotherapist went wrong. His making tea for you at the beginning of sessions was a crossing
of boundaries—an appeasement. The proof of this is in
his own words: you were "special." And the cruel things
he said to you throughout the treatment, in addition to
his ignoring your e-mails and "dumping" you, illustrate his
desire to harm you in retaliation for your anger.

These psychotherapeutic mistakes had clear consequences
for you. First, they gave you hope that, in being special,
you might not lose his approval. Second, they pushed you
into thoughts that, through a sado-masochistic relationship, you might win his approval.

In the end, then, you didn't really fall in "love" with
him, you became enamored of the hope that you might,
through your own efforts, overcome his anger at you. This
isn't being uplifted to the level of love, it's being reduced to
the level of your own childhood trauma.

By that last statement I mean that, because of his own unrecognized counter-transference issues, your psychotherapist did not provide psychotherapy to you; instead, he merely recreated the original trauma of your childhood: a parent who both abused you and appeased you but failed to understand your true emotional needs.

Now, as you yourself have remarked, the prospects of your finding help in the mental health system are bleak. Nevertheless, even though you lack the funds to pay for competent private care, you still have one option. You could use your desire for spiritual healing to lead you into a discovery of true love. Through personal study and meditation you could find that place where, rather than constantly feeling frustrated by the failures of the world around you, and trying impossibly to satisfy your need for approval from others, you can learn to acknowledge openly your emotional wounds. Then, rather than react with rage and retaliation, you might give to others your expression of profound emotional qualities such as patience, compassion, understanding, and forgiveness. In this way, you will find what you have been seeking all your life: real love.

I am a highly functioning depressed borderline [BPD].
I've been to over 20 psychotherapists in 20+ years. I feel
confident that I'm just smarter than a lot of psychotherapists I meet (I often know more than the psychotherapist
about issues and techniques germane to my situation; I
am often more seasoned than the psychotherapist; when
I do get defensive I can kill the effectiveness of the psychotherapeutic session because the psychotherapist isn't
strong enough to bring us back to what I'm avoiding).
When I felt feelings for my current psychotherapist,
I told her I believed we should really examine it, this
transference thing that feels so much like unrequited
love. I don't think she's capable of understanding, or
maybe just not of dealing with what I'm going through.
Transference exists, it is part of the process and is rightly
acknowledged.

But what happens in a psychotherapeutic crush (such
as mine) is more than that. For one, it is a rock solid ob-
servation that this psychotherapist has presented all of
the behaviors, talents and intellect that, in a friendship,
would give me the righteous and healthy connection
I crave when those with whom I do connect leave me
grateful but bored and empty. And two, this transference is a wish for a metaphysical impossibility, the urge
to merge, the urge to disappear into someone who could
be me for me, to relieve me of the burden while I delight-
ed in an ultimate closeness at a molecular level.

Given that I have such a hard time finding psychotherapists, I am truly loathe to abandon this one. In the
past few months I have started to use the word "trust"

with her. That took two years. When I read your notes to writers about their transference, your depth of knowledge and instruction that transference should be examined over and over left me sure that I would not be able to work through my transference with this psychotherapist because she just can't handle it. I also must say that I really appreciate having you to write all of this to. I don't know of any other outlet, and writing this letter feels quite satisfying, both for getting it out and for knowing that I will be heard by someone who really understands the transference issues.

First of all, you give a very accurate description of the illusions of common love. These illusions not only cause many interpersonal problems, but they often lie at the core of many mental health problems as well.

Moreover, a central dynamic of BPD is rage—rage about not getting from others the seeming satisfaction of common love.

So, since you value my opinions so highly, I will get right to the point here and tell you the truth: although you are a very smart person, your intellect has fooled even you and has become a weapon of rage. Essentially, early in life your intellect developed ingenious psychological defenses to protect you from emotional pain, but as you got older, those very defenses, created to protect you, began causing interpersonal conflicts that have been holding you back from using the full potential of your intellect. Now you're in the sad predicament of offending others even as you try to protect yourself.

In fact, paying me a compliment is an underhanded way of throwing an insult to your current psychotherapist.

What, then should you do? Well, if would be helpful if you were to learn humility, the antidote to pride. It will be important to shatter the illusions of common love and discover real love because real love is the ability to seek the good of another without regard for your personal satisfaction or gain. Moreover, this real love does not depend on being smart; it's simply a humble, honest human interaction with psychologically healthy boundaries.

So it will be important to stop using your intellect to fight the world because of what you're not getting from the world, and, instead of rage, to give to the world what you have never received: real love.

Furthermore, because it won't be easy to find a psychotherapist smarter than you are, go back to your current psychotherapist and teach her real love by your willingness to allow her to teach you humble, illusion-free trust and honesty.

INDEX

Abandonment, fear of, 33

Abuse, 8, 13, 23, 24, 32, 43,
   49, 51
   of power, 56
   physical abuse, 8, 30
   putting up with, 43
   sexual, 8, 49, 51

Abused, 12, 24
   children, 8

Abusing alcohol, 16

Abusing the truth, 28

Admitting the truth, 22, 23

Afraid, 13

Alcohol, abusing, 16

Anger, 10, 13, 22, 24, 30, 39,
   41, 43, 46–48, 52–56

Angry, 13

Anxiety, 29, 38, 52

Appeasing, 55
   a parent, 28
   others, 32

Auscultation, 47

Authority, 14

Being genuine, 34

Being nice, 33, 34

Belief that you are worthless, 9

Betrayal of the truth, 28

Blame, 21, 22, 23, 24, 25, 29
   letting go of, 25

Blaming your parents, 25

Body, 16

Borderline Personality Disorder, 54, 55, 58, 59

Boundaries, 7, 8, 10–14, 17, 20,
   29, 30, 31, 35, 37–41, 43, 44,
   46–49, 51, 55, 56, 60

BPD, 54, 55, 58, 59

Breaking a promise, 28

Breaking the law, 14

Broken promise, 28

Bullying, 20

Capitulating, 10

Causing the loss of someone's
     time, 27
Caustic persons, 34
Charity, 10, 11
Cheated, 22
Child abuse, 8
Childhood, 7, 8, 9, 12
     trauma, 56
Children, 8
Cigarettes, 16
Cigarette smoke, 16
Clinical judgment, 38
Clothing, 16
Common love, 42, 43, 59, 60
Compassion, 22, 42, 57
Condemnation, 13
Conflicts, 18
Control, being in, 42
Controling the behavior of
     others, 17
Counter-intuitive principles, 35
Courage, 8
Criticizing, 32
Curse, 36
Cynicism, 47

Defense mechanisms, 7, 8
Demands, 35
Denial, 24
Denying the truth, 23

Depression, 38, 39
Deserve, to, 9, 13
Desperation to feel accepted, 43
Dignity, 7, 8, 12, 13, 16, 25
Dishonesty, 8
Disorder, 11
Distress, 27, 29
Drugs, 16
Duped, 22
Dysfunctional, 36
     behaviors of others, 30
     families, 10, 28, 32, 39
     relationship, 42–44

Eating disorder, 40, 42
Emotional conflicts, 46
Emotional harm, 7
Emotional healing, 22
Emotional manipulation, 8
Emotional pain, 21, 24
Emotional wounds, 22, 43, 47,
     55, 57
Empathy, 24
Enemy of love, 34
Entitlement, 20
Ethics, 12

Facts of your childhood, 25
Failing to keep a promise, 28
Family, 10, 15

Family role, 10
Fear, 8, 10–13, 29–31
Feeling understood, 36, 37
Forbearance, 11, 22
Forgiveness, 22, 44, 57
Foul language, 11, 19
Free will, 31

Game, rules of a, 14
Gentleness, 19
Genuine, being, 34
Good, the, 15
Growth, 25
Guidance, 15
Guilt, 31, 43

Harm, 7
Hate, 13, 24
Hatred, 12, 13, 14, 24
   for the self, 12
Healing, 21, 22, 23, 24, 25
Health, 16
Helplessness, 42, 56
Hiding anger, 13
Hiding the truth, 23
Honesty, 25, 60
Honoring parents, 32
Hoping for love, 32
Hostility, 10
Humility, 60

Hurt, 8, 10, 12
Hurting someone's feelings,
   29, 30

"I am not worthless", 9
"I'm not going to argue with
   you about it", 18
Imperfect childhood logic, 12
Imprudence, 26
Independence, 36
Indignity, 16
Individuality, 16
Infancy, 35, 36
Infant development, 35
Injustice, 22
Insult, 8
Insulted, 13
Integrity, 12
Irrational outbursts of anger,
   30
"It's none of your business", 18

Justice, 25

Keeping a promise, 28

Lack, 8, 9, 12
Language, 11
Law, breaking the, 14
Letting go of blame, 25

Lies, 33
Logic, 9, 12
Love, 10, 11, 15, 32–34, 37, 42–45, 52, 54, 56–60

Making others love you, 32
Manipulation, 8, 14, 15, 31, 32, 42, 44
Manipulative, 8
Mature confidence, 36
Mental health problems, 59
Mercy, 22
Mistakes, 24, 25
Mistreated, 12, 13
Mistreatment, 9, 13
Moral values, 15
Mutual cooperation, 7

Needs, 15, 16, 35–37
Negative belief, 9
Nice, being, 10, 33, 34

Offender, 13
Offensive text messages, 19
Office procedures, 14

Pain, 21, 23, 24
Parents, 13, 21, 23, 25
Parental failures, 25
Past, the, 8

Patience, 22, 42, 57
Paying the price, 14
    for healing, 21
Peace, 10
    keeper, 10
Personal example, 11
Physical abuse, 8, 30
Positive belief, 9
Pressured, 15
Private matter, 17
Problem children, 33
Promise, 26, 28
Protecting yourself, 17
Protection, 9
Protest, 22
Psychological change, 23
Psychological defenses, 7
Psychological limit, 7
Psychotherapy, 36, 37

Rage, 43, 44, 54, 55, 57, 59, 60
Real love, 44, 57, 60
Refusing to hate, 13
Repent, 13
Resentment, 22–25
Resistance, 8, 9
Respect, 26
Responsibility, 20, 21, 23–30
Responsible, 20, 23, 24, 26–28
    for the feelings of others, 20

Restraint, 31
Retaliation, 55, 56, 57
Revenge, 55
Romantic fantasy, 42
Rude, 8, 10, 11
Rudeness, 11, 18
Rules, 14, 15

Sabotage, 8
Sacrifice, 10
Sarcastic, 19
Saying "No", 17
Seduction, 42, 43, 46
Self-doubt, 39
Self-hatred, 13
Selfishness, 15
Self-loathing, 21
Self-punishment, 21
Self-sabotage, 8
Sexual abuse, 49, 51
Shame, 30, 31
Shaming, 30
Shirking responsibility, 29, 30
Smoking, 16
Social context, 14
Social compensation, 22
Sorrow, 21, 23, 24
"Spill your guts", 15
Spiritual liability, 21
Stating facts, 25

Stifling, 32
Suffering, 21, 25
Suicide, 21
Sulking, 30
Survival, 8

Taking blame for behaviors of
    others, 30
Temptation, 28, 35, 36
Terrorism, 20
Touched, to be, 16
Transference, 40, 48, 52, 57–59
Trauma, 56, 57
Truth, 21, 22, 23, 28, 30, 32, 33
    abusing, 28

Unconscious, 8, 10, 22, 23, 25,
    39, 41–44, 46, 47, 50, 55, 56
    anger, 39
    core of problems, 39
unconsciously motivated, 7,
    11, 31
Unethical, 48
Unfair, 22
Unworthy, 9

Values, 18
Victim, 21–23
    anger, 22
    mentality, 39

Victimization, 21
Vulnerability, 42

Walking on eggshells, 29
Warning, giving a, 13
Worthless, feeling, 9, 13
Wounds, emotional, 43

Welling, 19

ABOUT THE AUTHOR

Raymond Lloyd Richmond, Ph.D. earned his doctorate in clinical psychology and is licensed as a psychologist (PSY 13274) in the state of California. He completed a Post-doctoral Fellowship in Health Psychology.

Previous to his doctoral degree, he earned an M.A. in religious studies, an M.S.E. in counseling, and an M.S. in clinical psychology.

During the course of his education he received specialized training in Lacanian psychoanalysis, psychodynamic psychotherapy, cognitive-behavioral therapy, and hypnosis.

His clinical experience encompasses crisis intervention; treatment for childhood emotional, physical, and sexual abuse; trauma and PTSD evaluation and treatment; and treatment of psychotic, mood, and anxiety disorders.

Made in the USA
Coppell, TX
28 May 2020

26619687R00039